The Lyfe of Saynt Radegunde

T0364333

The Lyfe of
Saynt Radegunde

Edited

from the copy in Jesus College Library

by

F. BRITTAIN, M.A.
of the same College

CAMBRIDGE
AT THE UNIVERSITY PRESS
1926

CAMBRIDGE
UNIVERSITY PRESS

University Printing House, Cambridge CB2 8BS, United Kingdom

Published in the United States of America by Cambridge University Press, New York

Cambridge University Press is part of the University of Cambridge.

It furthers the University's mission by disseminating knowledge in the pursuit of
education, learning and research at the highest international levels of excellence.

www.cambridge.org
Information on this title: www.cambridge.org/9781107415928

© Cambridge University Press 1926

First published 1926
First paperback edition 2014

A catalogue record for this publication is available from the British Library

ISBN 978-1-107-41592-8 Paperback

Introduction

The copy of *The Lyfe of Saynt Radegunde* which is here edited is to be found in the library of Jesus College, Cambridge, and has the following inscription on the fly-leaf:

"C & P[1]

"July 3d 1792.

"Dr. Farmer Master of Emanuel presents this Book to the "Library of Jesus College. It formerly belonged to the famous "Tom. Rawlinson, & lately to that great Collector, Major "Pearson. Dr. Farmer has been for many years inquisitive after "Pieces of this sort & he does not know, that another copy "exists in the World."

Largely, no doubt, on the strength of Doctor Farmer's statement, this copy has hitherto been believed at Cambridge to be the only one in existence, though there is at least one other. Curiously enough, this other copy was also considered by its possessors to be unique, and its present owner in all probability still thinks that it is so, as the Jesus copy has never appeared in any lists of early printed books.

The earliest mention of the second copy occurs in the 1785 edition of *Typographical Antiquities* by William Herbert, who states that it is in his possession. After passing through various collections into the celebrated Britwell library, it was sold at Sothebys in 1922, being purchased by an American firm for £295. No other copies are known to exist.

Richard Pynson[2], the printer of *The Lyfe of Saynt Radegunde*, was a Norman who learned his craft in France and migrated to London some time before 1490. In 1508 he succeeded William Faques as King's Printer, and in the following year introduced at the end of his books a full-page engraving, the

---

[1] Rawlinson's mark for "collated and perfect"
[2] Cf. E. G. Duff, *Printers of Westminster and London from 1476 to 1535* (Cambridge, 1906).

use of which some years later by the printer Redman caused
a fierce dispute between Pynson and his rival.

This engraving is the one used by Pynson at the end of
Saynt Radegunde and reproduced in the present edition.
Some of the figures in it have no satisfactory explanation.
It is difficult to identify the bird above the shield. In
previous devices used by Pynson the bird had a shorter
bill, and was probably intended to represent a finch (*pinson*).
Herbert describes the sprig in its beak as "with two mul-
berries, as described by Guillam, but appearing rather like
the cones of a pine." The latter seems the more natural explanation, and is also the more probable, as it would introduce a
pun on Pynson's name.

Pynson resigned the office of King's Printer in 1529, and
died early in 1530. Since he is described in the colophon to
Saynt Radegunde as "printer to the kynges noble grace," the
book must have been published not earlier than 1508 and not
later than 1529. As Pynson published, as far as is known,
only three small legal works after 1527, the probable limits
may be reduced to 1508 and 1527.

The author of *The Lyfe of Saynt Radegunde* is not named
on the title-page or in the text. The only detail which he gives
about himself is that he was

> "lowest of degre
> A man of holy church by true profession."

The work which most nearly resembles the present one in
metre, style, and general treatment is *The Lyfe of Saynt
Werburge*[1], by Henry Bradshaw[2], about whom very little is
known except that he was a Benedictine monk at the abbey
of St Werburge in his native city of Chester; that he was sent

---

[1] Edited by C. Horstmann (London, E.E.T.S., 1887); also by E.
Hawkins (Chetham Soc., 1848).
[2] Cf. Anthony à Wood: *Athenae Oxonienses* (ed. P. Bliss, London, 1813),
vol. 1.

by the community to study theology at Gloucester College, Oxford; that on his return to Chester he wrote *The Lyfe of Saynt Werburge*; and that he died in 1513, probably prematurely, and was buried in his monastery, "leaving then behind him others matters to posterity."

The resemblance between *Saynt Werburge* and *Saynt Radegunde* was noticed by Herbert, and is indeed very striking. Both are written in "rhyme royal" stanzas of seven lines. Only ten stanzas in *Saynt Radegunde* depart from this rule, each of them having eight lines. One of these stanzas is isolated, the extra line being in Latin. The other nine together comprise the penultimate chapter, the eighth line of each forming a refrain. *Saynt Werburge* has some eight-line stanzas for similar purposes and in similar positions, and their proportion to the whole poem is about the same as in *Saynt Radegunde*.

In addition to their similarity in construction, rhyme, and slip-shod style, the two poems offer a very close parallel in language and method of procedure, even in small details. Both saints are described as "a myrour of mekenes," "a lanterne of lyght," "kynges doughter dere," "circumfulsed with grace," and compared to the rose. Each is implored to deliver man from "paynes thrall," and the carnal desire of both their husbands is extinguished "as water quencheth the fyre." Each is invoked by the author in a brief prayer for inspiration at the end of the prologue, as also in a longer prayer just before the epilogue. The wedding festivities of Radegund are described in detail, as are those at the spiritual marriage of Werburge. Each saint sends for her sisters on her death-bed, gives them advice, and utters a lyrical "welcom" to the Viaticum. In both poems the nuns lament the death of the saint, and pray God to restore her to life. The soul of both saints is received by angels, who conduct it to Paradise. Each poem opens with an astronomical introduction, is submitted to the judgement "of all poetes," is stated to have been written to avoid idleness, and for the benefit of the common people, not of the learned. Further, in both poems Chaucer, Lydgate, Skelton and Barclay are mentioned, but no other English poets.

Even after due allowance has been made for the commonplaces used by hagiographers in all ages, and by English poets in the late fifteenth and early sixteenth centuries, the resemblance between the two poems is still so very close that one can only conclude that Bradshaw wrote both of them.

Bradshaw's ability as a poet has been variously estimated. Warton remarks that his versification "is infinitely inferior to Lydgate's worst manner," and that he had "more piety than poetry." Dibdin[1], on the other hand, considers that "his name will stand among the foremost in the list of poets of his period"; while Horstmann praises his "attempt at epic style," and states that he "generally retains the old popular long-line used by the Anglo-Saxons." Professor Saintsbury, however, says that "it has been charitably suggested that, in place of Chaucerian decasyllables, Bradshaw retains the 'old popular long line,' whatever that may be. To which it can only be replied that if he did not mean decasyllables he constantly stumbles into them. If he is not quite so shambling as some of his predecessors and contemporaries, he is, throughout, steadily pedestrian."

A passage in *Saynt Werburge* implies that that poem was finished in 1513, the year of its author's death. It is highly probable, therefore, that *Saynt Radegunde*, if we assume that Bradshaw wrote it, is the earlier of the two. This supposition is strengthened by a comparison of the two poems, as *Saynt Werburge* is four times as long, is more mature in style, and has a structure which seems in many ways to be an expansion

---

[1] *Typographical Antiquities* (London 1812), vol. II, p. 499.

of *Saynt Radegunde*. As Bradshaw undoubtedly regarded *Saynt Werburge* as his life's work, its composition may have occupied him for several years. If that be so, *Saynt Radegunde* may well have been written about 1500, or earlier.

It is difficult to say why Bradshaw should have chosen Saint Radegund as the subject of a poem, as we have no evidence that he ever lived in any of the few places in England where a church is dedicated to her. It is not likely that he visited her shrine at Poitiers, or he would almost certainly have mentioned the fact in his poem.

Pynson printed several works by Bishop Alcock of Ely. Yet, although the name of Saint Radegund is now inseparable at Cambridge from that of Alcock, there is no evidence that the bishop had any special devotion to her. What evidence there is points in the contrary direction, since, when Alcock converted the nunnery of Saint Radegund into a college, he wished to change its dedication entirely. If therefore, as is possible, he met Bradshaw through the medium of Pynson, he is hardly likely to have suggested the life of Saint Radegund as the subject of a poem.

Yet the suppression of the Benedictine community of Saint Radegund at Cambridge must soon have become known to the Benedictines of Chester, and the reasons which led Bishop Alcock to order its suppression must have formed the subject of more than one hour's surmise and gossip among the monks at the abbey. Listening to it, and doubtless taking part in it, Henry Bradshaw would realise that he could do nothing to alter what had taken place, but that he could at least do something to perpetuate the memory of the saint whose name the nuns of Cambridge, and the Benedictines as a whole, had so long venerated. He could hope, moreover, to find a sympathetic publisher in Pynson, to whom, as a Norman, the cult of Saint Radegund was probably already well known, as his native province contains several churches dedicated to her.

Saint Radegund[1] is a strictly historical character of the sixth century, and was born about the year 520 in Thuringia[2], of which her father, Berthaire ("Berengary") was joint ruler with his two brothers. In the year 531 she was taken prisoner of war by Clotaire ("Lothary"), the youngest son of Clovis, removed to his court at Athies, and forced to marry him at an early age. After several years of married life she left her husband, and was consecrated a deaconess by Saint Medard, Bishop of Noyon. Judging by what is known of Clotaire's character, she was fully justified in leaving him. Shortly afterwards, she founded at Poitiers a double community of monks and nuns, who followed the Cesarian Rule until long after their foundress's death. Not long before her death in 587, Radegund received a vision of Christ, who appeared to her in the form of an angel. This visit is the subject of the engraving prefixed to *The Lyfe of Saynt Radegunde*. She was buried in the monastic church, where her tomb still attracts large numbers of pilgrims from all parts of France.

The cult of Saint Radegund was introduced into this country long before the Norman Conquest. Winchester was one of its earliest centres, and the New Minster there, like Glastonbury, possessed relics of the saint. The earliest written mention of her name on this side of the Channel occurs in a calendar written by a priest of Winchester probably about the middle of the ninth century. It is to Winchester also that we probably owe an eleventh-century copy of the Missal of Robert of Jumièges, in the calendar of which we find the name of Saint Radegund. We find it also in the Leofric Missal, written before the Conquest for use in Exeter cathedral; in the *Calendarium Anglicanum*, and in the missals of Ely and Hereford. It does not appear in the Sarum calendar, though

---

[1] Cf. F. Brittain, *Saint Radegund, patroness of Jesus College* (Cambridge, 1925).

[2] The author of *The Lyfe* had vague ideas about "Thorynga," which he makes an African city in the kingdom "now called Barbarea." This is due to his mistranslation of the original, "haec natione barbara fuit."

Salisbury cathedral possessed "the heer of Seint Radegunde" among its "relikes of virginys."[1]

In practically every one of these early missals and calendars we find the saint commemorated, not on August 13th, the anniversary of her death, but on February 11th. This feature is peculiar to England. Not even a minor feast of the saint is kept on February 11th elsewhere.

The Norman Conquest gave little, if any, impetus to the cult in England, but the reverse is true of the Plantagenet period, largely owing to the close feudal connection between England and Poitou from Henry II's marriage with Eleanor of Aquitaine in 1152 until the English were driven out in 1369. It is significant that every English church or chapel dedicated to Saint Radegund received its dedication, so far as can be discovered, during the Plantagenet period.

It is somewhat surprising to find that, although the number of dedications to Saint Radegund in England is comparatively small, it exceeds that in any other country except France and Austria. The actual number of English dedications is twelve, five of these being parish churches, three monastic houses (at Bradsole in Kent, Thelesford in Warwickshire, and Cambridge), two cathedral side-chapels (St Paul's and Exeter), one monastic side-chapel in the Benedictine nuns' priory at Usk[2] in Monmouthshire, and one bath, at Canterbury, which may possibly owe its name to Bertha, wife of Ethelbert of Kent, who was a grand-daughter of Clotaire.

The cult of Saint Radegund spread at an early date into Wales, and her name appears in the Martyrology of Ricemarch, drawn up for use at St David's between 1076 and 1081. It is, however, possible that the commemoration was inserted at a later date[3].

[1] Chr. Wordsworth, *Ceremonies of the Cathedral Church of Salisbury* (Cambridge, 1901), p. 40.

[2] *Monasticon Anglicanum*, ed. Caley, 1823, vol. IV, p. 592, col. 1.

[3] H. J. Lawlor, *Psalter and Martyrology of Ricemarch* (Bradshaw Soc. 1914), vol. I, pp. xxi, xxxiii.

That the cult had spread as far as Ireland by the latter part of the twelfth century is shown by the inclusion of Saint Radegund's name in the Martyrology of Gorman, a rhymed calendar in Erse, composed some time between 1166 and 1174[1]. In this instance the commemoration falls on August 13th, and is rather prettily worded:

> "Radicuind noem nuaghel
> (Holy, fresh-fair Radegund)."

There are a few instances of the use of the saint's name after the Reformation in England. In the parish of Bengeworth, Worcestershire, children of both sexes were christened by the name of Radegund as late as 1580, or thereabouts, as can be seen from the parish registers[2]. The Amazonian queen in Spenser's *Faerie Queene*, although utterly different from the saint in character, is named "Radigund." The same writer sums up a few of the saint's characteristics in his *Mother Hubberd's Tale* (1591).

Of Laurence Sterne's references to the saint in *Tristram Shandy* (1761), one is a mere ejaculation, but the other shows that Sterne knew the details of the saint's austerities. This passage refers to the metal cross, armed with sharp points, which Radegund used to heat in the fire and apply to her flesh. The nuns of Poitiers do not claim to possess this relic. They appear to have made such claims formerly, but a recent writer has shown conclusively that the cross in their possession could not have been the one used for the purpose described. It is quite possible, however, that the community "in your road from Fesse to Cluny" who are said to have shown the relic to Tristram may have possessed it in Sterne's time, and that he saw it, though its existence is unknown to-day.

We are exceptionally well provided with contemporary Latin accounts of the life of Saint Radegund. The first of

---

[1] W. Stokes, *Martyrology of Gorman* (Bradshaw Soc. 1895), pp. xix and 156.

[2] *Notes and Queries*, vol. cxlix, p. 196.

these was written by the chaplain to her community, Venantius Fortunatus, whose biography of the saint was afterwards supplemented by the nun Baudonivia. Much additional information is to be found in the works of Gregory of Tours, who frequently visited the community and officiated at the funeral of its foundress. In the eleventh century Hildebert, Bishop of Mans, compiled a life of the saint, but it is little more than an abstract and re-arrangement of the matter contained in the biographies by Fortunatus and Baudonivia.

None of these writers is mentioned by the author of *The Lyfe of Saynt Radegunde*. This is because, although he used some of the information given by all four of them, he used it for the most part indirectly, through another channel—the works of Antoninus, who is the only writer about Saint Radegund whom he mentions by name.

This Antoninus, in order to distinguish him from other writers of the same name, is generally referred to as Antoninus of Florence, in which city he was born in 1389, and of which he became Archbishop some years before his death in 1459. His chief work is his Latin *Chronicle*, a summary of the history of the world down to the year before his death. Two sections of this work are devoted to the life of Saint Radegund[1], and are admittedly taken from the works of the indefatigable encyclopaedist, Vincent of Beauvais. Except for the omission of two or three short passages, and the alteration of a word here and there, Antoninus follows Vincent word for word in his biography of Saint Radegund. Neither of them includes more than a few words from Gregory of Tours. They are practically content to give a mere summary of Fortunatus and Baudonivia, whom they follow verbatim whenever possible.

The author of *The Lyfe of Saynt Radegunde* follows Antoninus very closely, and about a third of the poem is

[1] Antoninus Florentinus, *Chronicorum Secunda Pars* (Lugduni, 1586), pp. 292–4.

taken directly from his work. In only three instances (and those very minor ones) does he change the order of events followed by the Italian writer; and he omits only four brief passages from the original Latin. None of these is of any note, with a single exception, which refers to an important event in the saint's life. It tells how her innocent brother was murdered by Clotaire—an event which rightly caused her to leave him and led to her taking the veil and founding her monastery. The English writer implies that her final resolution to seek the monastic life was made owing to the noising abroad of her first miracle. He probably thought that a husband's consent was all that a married woman needed to set her free for the monastic life, and that there was consequently no need to mention the murder, though it is that very incident which makes Radegund appear a much more human figure to the modern reader.

The narrative of Antoninus is supplemented in the poem by eleven incidents or passages drawn direct from Fortunatus, six from Baudonivia, three from Hildebert, and by the account of the Legend of the Oats, which comes from a much later source. These borrowings put together are not equal to a third of the amount which is translated from Antoninus.

Nearly half of the poem is the original work of the English writer, even though he refers to it as a "poore translacion." The prologue and epilogue are original, as are the descriptions of Radegund's wedding and profession, her address to her sisters from her death-bed, her reception of the last sacraments, her "welcom" to the Viaticum, the lengthy account of how she kept her virginity, the summary of her miracles, a number of stanzas extolling her good example, and practically all the prayers.

In only two instances does the author do violence to his sources. Otherwise, he merely adds graphic touches which undoubtedly give more life to the poem than is contained in the Latin biographies. The two exceptions lie in his special pleading to prove the virginity of Radegund after her marriage, and in his constant references to her as "abbasse." On both these points he conforms to mistaken views which grew up during the later Middle Ages, and is at variance with all early writers about the saint, including Hildebert in the eleventh century.

The Legend of the Oats, which furnishes the most picturesque incident in the poem, is based on a late tradition which is first found in a French manuscript of the fourteenth century. The same story is given in a Latin manuscript, *Nova miracula beate Radegundis*[1], of the fifteenth century, which was probably the source used by the English writer.

There exist a number of Romance folk-tales and ballads which bear a striking resemblance to the story of Saint Radegund and the oats. One of these is contained in the fifteenth-century mystery play, *Le Geu des Trois Roys*[2], and treats of an incident during the flight of the Holy Family into Egypt. A very similar story is related in the Catalan ballad, *El rey Herodes*[3]; in two Franco-Provençal carols[4] from the district of Velay; in a ballad from Roussillon[5]; in a Breton legend of Saint Cornelius[6]; in a Poitevin prose legend of Saint Macrine[7]; and in another prose legend from the same province, *Le Conte du Diable*[8], which relates how two children escaped the pursuit of the devil through the miraculous growth of a crop of oats.

The legend of Saint Radegund and the oats is therefore but one form of a folk-tale which is perhaps a Christian

[1] Ed. Largeault et Bodenstaff, *Analecta Bollandiana*, tom. xxiii.
[2] Text in Jubinal, *Mystères du 15me Siècle* (Paris, 1837), vol. ii, p. 79.
[3] Text in Milà y Fontanals, *Romancerillo catalan* (Barcelona, 1895), p. 116.
[4] Text in *Romania*, vol. viii, p. 418.
[5] Chauvet, *Légendes du Roussillon*, p. 95.
[6] Fouquet, *Légendes du Morbihan*, p. 98.
[7] Sébillot, *Gargantua dans les traditions populaires* (Paris, 1883), p. 173.
[8] Pineau, *Contes populaires du Poitou* (Paris, 1891), p. 135.

adaptation of pagan myths connected with the corn-spirit. At Poitiers, however, the legend is still accepted as genuine by many, and oats are offered at Saint Radegund's shrine in continuation of a custom of which written records can be traced back to 1303.

The author of *Saynt Radegunde* refers to diseases cured in this country "by offeryng of otes" to the saint. His words imply that paralysis was one of these. A passage in the *Nova Miracula* shows that paralysis was known as "Saint Radegund's disease" as early as 1306 in France.

The offering of oats to Saint Radegund, and the story of her escape from her husband, bear a resemblance to the legend of the mythical saint Wilgeforte, otherwise known as Saint Uncumber, this name being given her by women, says Sir Thomas More in his *Dialogue concernynge hereyses*, "bicause they reken that for a pecke of Otes she will not faile to vncomber them of their housbondes."

∴

This edition of *The Lyfe of Saynt Radegunde* corresponds word for word and letter for letter with the black-letter copy in Jesus College Library, except that the contractions in the original have been expanded into italics, and that what seemed to be obvious misprints have been corrected, the original readings being given in the footnotes. The page-headings have been added by the editor.

The punctuation—or the lack of it—has been left as in the original, as the text is sufficiently clear without any alteration in this respect. Only those words which may present difficulty have been explained in the footnotes. Words marked with an asterisk are not included in the *New English Dictionary*.

The editor's thanks are due to the Master and Fellows of Jesus College for their generous contribution towards the cost of publication, and also to the Syndics of the Press, without whose co-operation publication would have been impossible.

Contents

¶Here begynneth the lyfe of saynt Radegunde.

The Table

⫶ Howe blessed Radegunde deliuered a woman possessed with a fende from daunger and payne to helth and prosperite.

⫶ How a ratte was slayne without hand approchyng to hurt the vertuous labour of saynt Radegunde.

⫶ Howe saynt Radegund by prayer reuiued a laurell tre to burge & bryng fourth leaues without rote.

⫶ Howe saynt Radegunde by humble supplicacion restored a yong Nonne from deth to lyfe agayne.

⫶ How saynt[1] Radegund saued her seruants from perell of perisshynge / whiche brought a parte of the holy crosse from the emperour.

⫶ Of dyuerse myracles in generall / and howe this abbasse saued diuerse sicke persons from Ieopardy of deth.

⫶ Howe Radegunde thabbasse cured two sicke women from infirmite / vnto helth and prosperite.

⫶ How this abbasse healed dyuerse sicke women some from feuers / and som from vexacion of our gostly enemy.

⫶ Of the gostly visyon she had afore her infirmite & of the noble exhortacion she made to her systers in her sickenesse and payne.

⫶ With what pacience and deuocion lady Radegund receyued the blessed sacrament and extreme vnction afore her departure.

⫶ Of the departynge of this holy abbasse / & howe she appered the same houre to a noble prefect / curyng hym from sickenesse of his throte.

---

[1] PYNSON, *sayut*.

⊞ Howe she cured one of her company from punysshement
of fier / and howe she saued & healed many other by true
oblacion made to her with deuocion[1].

⊞ An orison made of the blessed Radegunde lady and abbasse.

⊞ A breue conclusion and end of this poore translacion
mouyng the reders to accept it symple though it be.

Finis.

[1] Here PYNSON omits one chapter-heading from the Table.

The Lyfe of Saynt Radegunde

℃ *The prologe of the translatour in the lyfe of mayden Radegunde | quene and princesse.*

WHan the feruent heate / of the somer season
Was almost endyd by course of nature
And Phebus entred þᵉ signe of Scorpion
Passing þᵉ equinoctial than ye may be sure,
The day decresed / þᵉ nyght dyd long endure
Cold frosty mornynges / and euintydes withall
Began to approche / a long space continuall.

That season lyueries ben vsed of duety
Ryght at the solempne feast of all Halomas
By the gentylnesse of England / and curtesy
To gladde theyr guestes / in euery lordes place
And to theyr company to be great solace
To passe the euentide / after good humanite
In myrthes / in disportes / and liberalite

Than I reuolued with due circumstaunce
The gentyll maners / and discrete behauour
Of seculer people vsyng temperaunce
How they dispend the tyme / the day / the houre
Some in great policy for wordly honoure
Some in marchaundise for lucre and wynnyng
And some in chiualry / great fame opteynyng

Some other gyuen to wanton company
To wordly pleasours / and singuler affeccyon
Some to distemperaunce and vile glotony
And some to Christes / labour / and occupacion

than, then   *lyueries*, entertainments, banquets   *of duety*, according to custom   *after good humanite*, in acts of kindness

yet some be disposed to contemplacion
To prayer to study / of theyr goodnesse
And some (the more pitie) to slouth / and ydelnesse

Now syth that I am lowest of degre
A man of holy church by true profession
Consyderyng the condicions of people worldly
(As afore is sayd) my fully entencion
By diuyne grace and gostly supportacion
Is for to wryte the lyfe historiall
Of Radegunde the princesse quene and moniall

After my reason me thynke more conuenient
To spende wynter nyghtes in suche besynesse
For drede of temptation and causles insolent
Rather than to lose suche tyme in ydelnesse
Whiche to all vyce / is rote and maistresse
Enuy to vertue / a stepmother to study
Occasyon of ruyne / and mycle malady.

A secondary cause / mouyng me thereto
To write the lyfe of this virgyn glorious
Was the instant desyre / and peticyon also
Of speciall frendes / honest and vertuous
Whiche lately requyred me full memorious
With synguler request / and humble instaunce
This lyfe to discrybe / with due circumstaunce

To whome I graunted / vnder this condicyon
That of their wysedom / they wolde excuse me
And take this poore dede / of no presumpcion
Nor done for vauntage / auoyding vaynglore
But alonly to content theyr mynde and satisfy
Where they knowe well my insufficience
My great ignoraunce / and also necligence

moniall, nun

The thyrde cause mouyng moste principally
Is for to extolle / the glorious name
Of this holy virgyn / and gracious lady
With honour / reuerence / and excellent fame
To the commen people / desiryng the same
Whose lyfe hath ben kept scilent many a day
Knowen to fewe persons within this countray

Therefore I require / and pray you euerychone
That this litell treatyse shall reed or se
To accept my mynde with your discrecion
And it to correct after your charite
Amende the mater / where is necessite
For syth it is knowen / that I am no clarke
Under protestacion / I procede to warke

And where I unworthy / this treatyse begyn
I humble beseke our blessed sauyour
His mother also mary the virgyn
To be my helpe / comfort / and succoure
Now sweete Radegunde / of virgins the floure
Make supplicacion / vnto the trinite
And direct my penne to describe thy stori

11.

℣ Of the progeny of saynt Radegunde and howe she
was taken in batell and maryed to Lothary
a kynge of Fraunce.

THe yere of our sauyour by full computacion
Fyue hundreth fully from the natiuite
As dyuers auctors makyn discripcion
Reyned in Fraunce in honour and ryalte
Two noble kynges / Childebert / and Lothary
Euery kyng knowing his parte and regyon
To them belonging / by ryght and custome

Childebert, third son of Clovis, died 558

At the same season / as sayth the history
A noble prince / reyned in Affrica
Named in cronicles kyng Berengary
Borne at a citie named Thorynga
Within the sayde kyngdome now called Barbarea
Which prince whylom [was][1] famous in renowne
Tyll that dame fortune vnfrendly put hym downe.

Whiche forsayd prince kyng Berengarius
Had in succession a noble princesse
A deuout lady / and a virgyn glorious
Nominat Radegunde / a gemme of holynesse
A floure of vertu / and a myrour of mekenesse
Whose gostly gouernaunce enduryng her lyfe
Unto all people may be a perspectyfe

This kynge Berengary by mysfortune in batell
Was piteously subdued / by kynges of Fraunce
His realme conqueryd / piteously to tell
Losing his honour / lande / and gouernaunce
And Radegunde taken / suche was her chaunce
By power remoued / from her land naturall
Amonge strangers to be continuall

Whan the kyng and the realme subdued were
And mayde Radegunde taken for a pray
Than the kynges of Fraunce for her in fere
Entended batell / whiche shulde haue the may
For she was beauteous and pleasant verray
Humble / gentyll / courtese / and moste fayre truly
yet she by lot fell / vnto kynge Lothary

For if Radegunde had nat delyuerd be
Great cruelte / besynesse / and vexacion

---

[1] Omitted by PYNSON

Had fortuned among kynges thre
Through great disdeyn / pryde / and ambicyon
For the realme of Fraunce in a triniall kyndome
Than was deuided cronicles do expresse
As the sequence of saynt Martyn doth reherse

This lady Radegunde / thus taken away
And by chaunce delyuered to kyng Lothary
Was brought with worship in to a countray
Callyd Veromandensis vnto the kynges citie
Nominat Atheras / to be kept in suertie
There to be norisshed / and haue refeccion
Doctryne and disciplyne / with hie discrecyon

℗ Kyng Lothary considering her gentilnesse
Her vertue / pacience / and proued wysdome
Her great humilite / constaunce / and sobernesse
Dayly encreasyng with augmentacion
Entended to mary spedely and soone
Lady Radegunde / and virgyn serene
To make her his spouses and louely quene

Unto this mariage and feast there was
Made great preparacion / and rialtie
The halles were hanged / with clothes of arras
Rychely embrodered / in ryall Imagery
The xii apostelles well set in degre
Martyrs / confessours / and virgyns withall
Were theyr purtered / with crowne victoriall

Ouer the syde tables curiously were wrought
Auncient histories of auctorite
Of patriarkes / and prophetes wisely outsought
Of the olde and newe testament set properly

Veromandensis, Vermandois, the district round St Quentin
and Noyon   *Atheras*, Athies, near Péronne

Histories were paynted of poetrie
Chambers were strawed with floures fragrant
Well dect with hangynges / fresshe / fayre / and vernant

This princesse was clad in clothes of golde
In sylkesse / veluettes / and tyssues fyne
A coronall was ordeyned richely to be holde
And crowned therewith / as christall dyd shyne
Set with ryall stones / the sapher celestyne
The diamont / the diadeke / the ruby / the topas
The carbuncle / the emerall / the perle theyr was

Lordes of the lande were redy present
Dukes / erles / barons / and knyghtes doughty
The commons assembled euer delygent
To gyue attendaunce as was theyr duety
The day was apoynted / of the matrimony
The chapell enowrned with mycle rychesse
The clergy attending at an houre expresse

℩ Kyng Lothary passed from his ryall palace
With many myghty peres and lordes of his lande
Radegunde hym folowed a princesse full of grace
With ladies many one the fearest coude befounde
They came to the chapell as we vnderstande
All thynge was prepared to that solempnite
Ornamentes and vestures of great ryaltie

The bysshop was redy / with his ministers all
To execute his office / of the said matrimony
The obseruauntes was done with honour ryall
The masse was songe / with mycle melody
With belles / and orgons / and solempne minstrelsy
The sacrament of spousage / was celebrat that day
With reuerence and worsship / in theyr best aray

*diadeke, a jewel resembling the beryl   enowrned, adorned

From thens they departed / to the kynges palace
The sayd kyng and quene / the lordes / and clergy
All thinges well ordered (as afore sayd was)
To attende in the hall marshalles were redy
Of meates and drinkes / theyr was great plentie
Veneson wildfoule mycle aboundaunce
The condites of wyne ranne with great pleasaunce

But for all this ryaltie / and wordly pleasure
Whiche was prepared / at this solempnite
The quene Radegunde passyng course of nature
Moste dredfull in hert / was for her virginite
Desyred our sauyour of his endlesse charite
As he for vs all suffred bitter[1] passion
To preserue her body from all corrupcion

III.

❧ *Of the vertuous lyuing of saynt Radegund*
undre spousage | and howe she con-
tynued a pure virgyne

WHan the day declyned & come was the nyght
And all people passyd echone to his lodgynge
The hert of Radegunde was litell of myght
yet priuatly she went to her chamber wepyng
Made great lamentacion dolefully sighing
Required our lorde to helpe of his pytie
To whome she had offred afore her virginite

Alas what tong can playnly expresse
Or hert may thynke / the dredfull Ieopardy
This lady Radegunde feared doutlesse
When her lorde was laid her swete body by

---

[1] PYNSON, *better*

Her soule was rapt / her mynde in an extasy
Plonged in heuenes / wo and penalite
More leuer to be deed / than lose her chastite

But as scripture sayth / our blessed sauiour
Is euer redy in extreme necessite
To helpe his seruantes both day and houre
Whan they do call / with pure humilite
He saued saynt Agnes / saynt Lucie / saynt Cecilie
With many other mo / from all corrupcion
Ryght so he preserued Radegunde that season

For whan Lotharias desired to supplie
Naturall pleasure and voluptious entention
By diuyne power and by myracle sothlie
His feruent desyre with carnall affeccion
Were clerly extincted for aboue reason
Suche frayle concupiscence of loue entyre
Soone seased as water quencheth the fyre

Other sondry seasons / whan the sayd kyng
Was moued at wyll / to haue his desiderye
The quene founde remedy / at her owne likyng
Sometyme feynyng sickenesse / and infirmite
Sometyme nat disposed to such fragilite
Sometyme occupied / in labours diligent
Other tyme obiectyng / the tyme nat conuenient

Thus by the grace / of her spouse Iesu
She euer preserued her true chastite
Geuyng her selfe / to prayer and to vertue
Lowyng our lorde / of his benignite
And his mother Mary / floure of virginite
Whiche of his mercy / and infinite goodnesse
Hath her preserued / in all distresse

for, far   *desiderye*, desire

And though she was maryed to kyng Lothary
A wordly prince / sekyng for honoure
She clerely refused / such pompe and vayne glory
And serued her spouse / our sauyoure
Transitory pleasurs / worship and decoure
Were truly abiected / and all suche felicite
More humble in wyll / than parmitted dignite

In wordly vanities / she had no pleasure
To gyue good example / was her hole entent
Sermons to here / was all her great cure
Loue and charite in hert were ay feruent
Her landes and rentes / geuen by assig[n]ment[1]
Were truly tithed / where was necessite
To captiue prisoners / and people in pouerte

All rentes / and richesse / that she myght com to
Were distribute to monasteris in deuocion
Besekyng the couent to pray for her also
And for her lorde / and all the region
Unto suche[2] places / as she myght nat come
By personall presence / for distaunce of place
Thyder she sende almys in short tyme and space

This noble quene had a principall mynde
Upon the poore people in great penalite
Shewyng werkes of mercy / acordyng to kynde
Helpyng all wofull wretchesse in miserie
Thynkyng all myspend / that they had nat truly
Beleuyng that Christ in euery poore creature
Lay secret and priue vnder theyr figure

Whan she was richely / serued at her table
With costly dayentes and delicacy
With myghty wyndes strong and comfortable
Conuenient for her estate and regalie

---

[1] PYNSON, *assigment*   [2] PYNSON, *snche*   *couent*, convent

With suche metes she nolde content her body
But dyd absteyne / and toke refeccion
With small potage of her owne decoccion

To punysshe her person / more strayte & sharply
Reuiuyng her sprite to meditacion
She ware the herd here / next to her body
With precious clothes reclothed ther vpon
Discrete abstinence / agaynst rebellion
Wysely oppressed / by the helpe of Iesu
Her corps makyng / apte to prayre and vertue

As Radegunde lay with her prince of right
She askyd lycence of a comyn custome
To depart and rise from bed euery nyght
For naturall necessite / acordyng to reason
From whome whan she was departed and gone
She went to prayer all nyght folowyng
Platte vpon an heer / on her knes knelyng

So with continuance / all the nyght season
Feruent in soule / to please god almyghty
Tyll her vitall sprite by true deuocion
Were almost confused / and put in Ieopardy
Thorowe colnesse frost / and all her body
From sensuall felyng of her wyttes fyue
Clerely were expulsed / by mynde contemplatiue

Wherefore it was sayd of her lorde and kyng
Of his true subgettes / and the comons all
That his noble lady / by gostly lyueng
Was nat as quene / but rather a moniall
The kyng her blamed in termes rurall
Reprouyng her customes / with great confusion
Whom she humble suffred without contradiccion

herd here, hard hair-shirt

IV.

*❡ Of the great deuocion she vsed namely in tyme of
lenton | and of the great pitie she had to
all captiue prisoners.*

WHan the tyme of lenton approched nere
To speke of her penaunce | is a strayte thyng
For at the same tyme | with conscience clere
She send to a religious woman in lyueng
Nominat Pia | her fully mynde sheweng
To whome this moniall | knowyng her entent
Send Radegunde an heer sealed full diligent

Whiche heer this lady (as rehersed is)
With reuerence receyued | and put next her body
Trustyng in the vesture great comfort and blis
Pleasaunt to our lorde | to her soule remedy
And yet she wolde were clothes richely
Upon the sayd heer in the tyme of lenton
Expellyng fame | and wordly commendacion

Upon solempne dayes | and feestes principall
The quene was reuest | with clothes of golde
With tissewes fyne | and veluettes at all
And whan the comon people | yong and olde
Praysed suche garmentes | with fame manyfolde
She vtterly abhorred | suche riall riche clothyng
Sende them to churches | for preestes in to syng

By fortune if Lothary her lorde were absent
Who wolde than byleue | her singuler deuocion
Her prayer | abstinence | and hert penetent
Her great contricion and humble supplicacion

---

a religious woman in lyueng, a woman living the religious
life, a nun   *reuest*, dressed

Euer remembryng our lordes passion
Submittyng her selfe as vnto his fete
Wasshesyng his woundes / with teares salt and wete

She refused glotony / by vertuous temparaunce
Our sauyour Iesu was her hole refeccion
Upon bodely feding / gaue litell attendaunce
Dayly prouidyng her soules sustentacion
Great vigilles / penaunce / and holy orison
Refresshed her soule / and the body also
No penaunce was tedious for her to do

If any transgressour were Iuged to dye
Or any man suffred wrong accusacion
She was so mercyable / and full of pitie
For them to the kyng / she made intercession
Knelyng full mekely / desyring peticyon
And to his counsell with prayer continuall
Tyll she had pardon / and grace for them all

All the kynges court / example myght take
To vse humilite / and great gentylnesse
At lady Radegunde / and synne to forsake
For why she was called / of more and of lesse
Rather a minister / than to be a maistresse
Deligent to serue / euery tyme and season
Pore / as well / as ryche with great deuocion

Nother man ne childe / dwellyng in the palace
Was discontent / at this swete lady
She had suche wysdome[1] / and singuler grace
Transcendyng other ladyes / of memory
Dukes / erles / and barons / and all theyr progeny
Example may take / at this quene ryall
To encrease in mekenesse / and vertuous morall

By her great prudence / and exortacion
The kyng was moued / to grace and pitie

---

[1] PYNSON, *wysdone*

Merciable to the pore / in all his region
Hauyng compassion / lyberall / and fre
To execute Iustice prompte with mercie
A good benefactour / to places religyous
By the instant mocion / of his quene vertuous

v.

❡ *Howe quene Radegunde shewed a great
myracle deliueryng prisoners
out of captiuite.*

THis noble quene euery solempne day
Of custome wolde ryse erly as the lyght
And go to her chapell / secretly to pray
Seruyng our sauyour / with all her hert and myght
Ensuyng mary Magdalayne in mynde full ryght
To mattens / and to masse / after she wolde gone
And all day folowyng vse meditacion

Thus by contynuaunce / in grace and goodnesse
In prayer / abstinence / vigils / and chastite:
This lady Radegunde / quene and princesse
Replete with mekenesse / vertue and charyte
Shewed dyuerse myracles / within the countre
The fyrst myracle / was done in the palace
(As saythe the history) by deuyne grace

As Radegunde passed the palace by a prison
Where many prisoners were fettred in durances
For her pastyme / solace / and consolacion
With lordes / knyghtes / and other seruantes
Whan the prisoners perceyued / beynge in penaunce
That it was the quene / theyr souerayne lady
With loude voyce / they began on her to call and cry

O noble princesse / O kynges doughter dere
O lady of grace / and quene imperiall

Succoure us thy seruantes whiche lye bounde here
Extende thy charite / vpon vs wretches all
Delyuer vs from deth / saue from paynes thrall
Be mercyfull to vs / hartfully we the pray
And we wyll amende our lyues / after this day

This lady heryng / suche great lamentacion
Inwardly was moued to mercy and pitie
Required to knowe / with tender compassyon
What people cryed on her so piteously
The seruantes answered agayne verite
Sayeng that they were beggers at the gate
Comon to haue almes of so great estate

Also the Iayler agayne all conscience
Rebuked his prisoners vnpiteously
Causyd them be styll / and kepe scilence
Manasing them to beate / punisshe / and mortyfy:
Conciled the truethe / from his souerayne lady
Thus the sayd prisoners / put to more payne
Had payne upon payne / without mercy certayne

But the next nyght folowyng / by myracle ryght
The fetters / the bondes / of the prisoners all
Sodenly were broken / and losed in theyr syght
And they were delyuered from paynes thrall
They passyng from prison / the gates downe dyd fall
They came the sayd nyght / to Radegunde theyr lady
Thankyng her echone / for her grace and mercy

They knelyd on kne / for gladnesse wepyng
Sayeng O souerayne lady / and maistresse
Honour be to the / grace and long lyueng
Whiche hath delyuered / vs from distresse
Personally this nyght / or els one in thy lykenesse
Nowe blessed Iesu / redemptour of vs all
Rewarde you this dede in the blysse eternall

agayne verite, PYNSON *agayne* (*verite*)

VI.

*❡ Howe quene Radegund desyred to be religyous | &
of a myracle shewed | at her departyng
by the way goyng*

WHIche myracle knowen this blessed lady
Made instant desyre / and humble supplicacion
To her husband / and lord kyng Lothary
That she myght haue lycense to go to religyon
Whose meke request / and singuler peticion
At last was graunted / with difficulte
Of the sayd kyng / to be at her lyberte

She lowed our lorde / in hert / worde / and dede
Of this fre graunt / and good expedicyon
She send to saynt Medard bysshop in good spede
Desyring hym for charite / and of his deuocyon
For to receyue her / in to holy religion
The place was apoynted / the tyme secretly
Of her comyng to Pictauis religious to be

In the meane whyle Radegund gaue to the poore
Moche ryall rychesse / and vestures liberally
Reseruyng to her person / and her vse no more
Than she dayly vsed / for honour necessary
So alone proceded / vnto the monastery
From the kynges court / priuely in the nyght
Unknowen to eche creature / saue to þe kyng of myght

Upon the other day / where the kyng perceyued
The sodayne departure of his lady sufferayne
He bitterly wayled / that he was disceyued
Sende dyuerse messangers / with a sure capitayne
Fyrst to enquire / and bringe her agayne
Supposyng to haue her / in short tyme and space
After she aproched / to the religious place

Pictauis, Poitiers

B   **2**

But the holy goost / confortour of all care
Defendyd Radegunde / at this extremite
For as she passyd / the fayre feldes all bare
She sayd to an husbande / besy in husbandry
People wyll folowe after / for to persue me
From whiche company I declyne certayne
Prayeng the consyle / my presens / and it layne

It behoueth the nat / from the trueth to verry
Say that thou see me come this same way
The season / day / and tyme / rennyng full hastely
Thou dyd sowe this corne affirmyng it verray
And thus excuse me / hertfully I the pray
She passyd this plowman / in to a secrete place
For drede truly[1] daryng / trustyng our lordes grace

Incontinently the corne newly cast in grounde
Began for to blade and bere in euery place
To eare and to rype (her enemyes to confounde)
All redy to be shorne / within an houre space
The otes began to shede / the husbande besy was
And made great prouision with sicle & sythe that morne
To cut downe the otes / in sauyng of the corne

After the sayd virgyn / messangers made great haste
Shortly to supple theyr lordes commaundement
They founde the husbande repyng corne full fast
Whome they required / to shewe on payne of prisonment
If any fayre lady / or mayde by hym went
To tell whan / and whyther / and whiche way þt she is
Auoydyng great displeasure / shewyng nat amys

Worshipfull maisters / the husbande than can say
Suche a fayre lady / we se this way gone
Rennyng fast and spedely the same selfe day

---

[1] PYNSON, *druly*   *husbande*, husbandman, peasant   *consyle*, conceal
it layne, be silent about it   *verry*, vary   *excuse me*, save me
from harm   *daryng*, trembling, crouching with fear   *can*, began to

That we cast this corne in the erth alone
Sweryng to them depely for more affirmacion
The courteours / beleued this honest man certayne
And heuely retourned to the kyng agayne

VII.

❡ *How Radegund was made relygious | & after elect*
abbasse of Pictauis | & howe by grace she was pre-
serued from daunger of her husbande þe kyng.

WHan nyght aproched / this forsayd fayre lady
Priuely departyd to the place of Pictauenȝ
Thankyng our lorde / and his mother Mary
Of her expedicion / with micle reuerence
The abbasse of the place gladed of her presence
So dyd the couent / and the company all
Of this noble quene / to be conuentuall

Mekely she made singuler peticion
To be religious vsyng lyfe monasticall
Thabbasse graunted / and the couent echone
Receyued her gladly / and made her a moniall
Where fyrst she layde asyde her purpull and pall
All riche vestures / of golde / and tissewes fyne
Her crowne / and coronall / set with stones celestyne

She was reclothed / with religious vesture
The mantell of mekenesse / the vaile of blacke colour
The wympull of wayling / of humble gesture
With other many vestures / of vertue that same hour
Thus for the loue of our sauyour
All wordly pleasures vayne / and transitore
She hath refusyd / obedient to be

heuely, heavily   *Pictauenȝ,* Poitiers   *wympull of wayling,*
wimple of wailing; cf. the prayer recited by a priest when vesting
for Mass: "Merear, Domine, portare manipulum fletus ac
doloris"

Whan the yere passed of her probacion
She truly professyd the essencials thre
Made a solempne vowe afore the congregacyon
Obedience to kepe also pure chastite
Enduryng her lyfe / with wilfull pouerte
She receyued the ryng / of heuenly spousage
Was maryed to Iesu enduryng this pilgrymage

And as myne auctour playnly doth expresse
The venerable Antoninus / in his historie
This lady Radegund / of her great goodnesse
Bylded afore tyme the sayd monastery
By the helpe of her husbande kyng Lothary
Where after she was elect lady and abbasse
By helpe of saynt Medarde a man of great grace

Whan she was abbasse / she toke to her company
A nomber of virgyns in hye perfeccion
To whome she gaue the example dayly
Of pure humilyte / and perfyt deuocyon
Of vertuous lyueng / and contemplacion
Perfourmyng in her persone / for goostly mede
All thyng commaunded / to her systers in dede

But the mortall enemy / of all mankynde
Consideryng in her / suche grace and vertue
By malyce / and enuy / forcast in his mynde
By some subtylte / this mayd to subdue
He tempted her husbande / a prince full of vertue
By power / and slouth to take his wyfe agayne
Out of religion / the more pyte certayne

This sayd kyng Lothary / in conscience blynde
Came with his company / to the citie of Turon
Under craft / and polesy prepensyd in mynde

essencials thre, the threefold vow of poverty, chastity, and obedience
wilfull, voluntary   *goostly mede*, spiritual reward   *Turon*, Tours

With the notable prince / Sygibert his[1] son
Dyssemblyng pylgrymage / and goostly entencion
Approchyng Pectauis / the rather that he myght
Take from religyon / his wyfe that same nyght

Whan Radegunde / herd[2] tell his subtell polysy
Howe he was paruerted as man without grace
She wept and wayled / in soule tenderly
For sorowe of her husbande / whiche somtyme was
In her hert no confort / was founde nor solace
For drede of deceyte / and ymagined treason
Prayeng to our lorde / for helpe that same season

She made secret letters / and send her entent
Closed and sealed / vnto saynt Garmayne
Bysshop of Parise / whiche than was present
With kyng Lothary / makyng her complaynt
Wofully lamenting / expressed in dede playne
Desiryng the bysshop / with humble supplycacion
To conuert the kyng / from his wrong opynion

Whan saynt Germayne these letters had reed
He prostrat hym selfe to the fete of the kyng
Afore saynt Martyns tombe prayeng hym in dede
By the order of charite / many salt teares wepyng
And for the loue of god / to conferme his askyng
That he no further / wolde procede in way
Nor come to Pectauis / for drede of deth that day

The kyng consideryng / in soule his great trespace
With bytternesse of hert / remembryng his peticion
Shulde come of Radegund / by singuler grace
With contrit hert and mynde / made playne confession
Excusing his defaute / by euyll suggestion
Prostrat his person vnto saynt Germaynes fete
Desiryng indulgence / with salt teares and wete

---

[1] PYNSON, *her*   [2] PYNSON, *hard*
Garmayne, Germain of Paris (A.D. 494–576)

Reputyng his presence / symple and vnworthy
For to call agayne his wyfe / from religion
Whiche is the spouse / of our lorde almighty
And vnder his licence entred professyon
Required the bysshop spedely to gone
To Lady Radegunde absoUed for to be
Lest punysshement fell on hym / soone and hastele

Whiche thynge the bysshop was glad for to do
Came to Pectauis / vnto her oratorie
And kneled at her fete / desiryng her also
To forgyue the kyng / his entent and miserie
Whiche thyng she dyd in hert / and worde gladly
Thankyng our lorde / that she was at lyberte
To serue hym day & nyght / delyuered from captiuite

VIII.

❡ *Of the feruent deuocyon of saynt Radegunde and
of the great penaunce and charitable
warkes she vsed in religion.*

WHat hert may thynke or tong is sufficient
To expresse the vertuous of this moniall
In deuout orison / in vigils conuenient
In discret abstinence / in vestures small
Example gyueng vnto her systers all
To the comon people / howe they in great vertu
Shulde dayly encrease / pleasyng our lorde Ihesu

This abbasse vsed silde / to eate whyte brede
But of rye or berly / kept secretly
That no man perceyued / howe that she fedde
Her drinke was water or little better dayly

symple, foolish

From her profession by saynt Medarde truly
Her repast was potage / and herbis for to eate
Nother fysshe / flesshe / egges / frutes / ne mylke meate

Also after the vsage / and rite of saynt Germayne
She had a litell mylne in her secret cell alon
In whiche all the lenton / she laboured certayne
As wolde well suffyce for iiii. dayes refeccion
A maruell howe she dyd satysfy euery person
Where nothyng wanted / that was necessary
The more that was gyuen / euer the more plenty

When obseruauntes were done / eche saturday at nyght
She toke a lynen cloth cloused about her body
And wasshed the heedes of all poore folkes aright
Rubbyng all theyr soris / sekenesse / and malady
She ayded and succoured / and dyd them remedy
After combyd them / or they passed the place
Nothyng abhorring suche mekenes in her was

To all poore creatures / the prouince round about
She euer ministred / the warkes of pytie
Gyuing to them clothyng / of almes without dout
Bothe lynen and wollyn / sytting for theyr degre
Whan they were greued / with any infyrmyte
She toke theyr vestures / and wasshed them echone
With her owne handes / after dyd them vpon

She send for poore folke / in her hall to dyne
Afore the ryche estates / for all theyr clothyng ryall
She serued the sayd poore / after Christis doctryne
Fyrst water to theyr handes / with a towell to them all
To persons impotent / she ministred speciall
Wasshyng theyr mouthes / theyr handes louingly
Suche was her custome / she was so full of pitie

mylke meate, foods prepared in milk or made from milk
obseruauntes the monastic Offices   *cloused*, wrapped   *or*, before

Whan all the seruyce / on the table was set
She wolde stande fastyng / to make them good chere
And deuyde theyr vitayls / as she myght get
Shewyng them good counsell theyr soulis to lere
All blynde / halte / and lame / to her were full dere
Whome with her handes / she fed with a spone
After gaue them drinke / with Christes benesone

Women full of lepre and vile corrupcion
In armes she wolde embrace / and kysse swetely
And gaue to them clothing / and refeccion
That many of them / were healed therby
Wherfore it was sayd / O thou swete lady
Who shall the kysse / or aproche the nere
Which kysses / such lepurs most vile in fere

IX.

☞ *Of the great perfeccion | and penaunce that lady
Radegunde vsed in the tyme
of lent.*

THis noble Radegunde / & venerable abbasse
All the tyme of lent after her profession
Whan she solitary in her cell set was
She absteyned from breed / & costly refection
Using herbis / potage / made of malous alone
Without oyle / and salt / except vpon the sonday
She toke brede alon / a lytell for that day

She absteyned so sore / from drinkyng of water
The XL. dayes of lent / with suche great penury
That she myght nat sing nor say with voyce clere
The seruice of god / nor orison priuatly

lere, instruct *fere*, health *malous*, mallows *myght*, could

She vsed the rough heer / next her tender body
Watchyng all the nyght / vsyng meditacion
Her bed was dry asshes / and an heer layed vpon

Her clothyng was so poore / symple and small
She had nat a sleue / vpon her armes to do
But of her hoses / she made twayne at all
To couer her from colde / from frost / and wynters wo
Thus she dyd punysshe / her propre body so
That she assembled a seruant for to be
Rather than an abbasse of great auctorite

Also whan her systers all in bed were layed
This lady Radegunde / wolde euery nyght
Wype clene theyr showes lyke a poore mayde
And with soft oyntment anoyent them full right
Make all thynge redy / agayne the day light
Of all vile labours / that a mong them there was
She wolde fyrst serue moost subget in the place

Wherefore as her cours / came wekely about
She swepped all places / of the monastery
All great vile burthens / she bare them out
From stretes and corners / fulsom for to se
Secret purgacions horible to the eye
She nothyng disdayned nor was dismayde
On her childers to cary (in story as is sayd)

She humbled her selfe as lest in degre
Bearyng wod to the fyre / in her armes twayne
Seruyng her systers vexyd with infirmyte
Preparyng sustentacion / meate and drynke certayne
Wasshyng theyr fysnamy / and fedyng them playne
Sundry tymes kyssyng them with great humilyte
Therby recoueryng dyuers from penalite

assembled, resembled, seemed   *showes*, shoes   *fulsom*, loathsome
*childers, shoulders   *lest*, least, lowest

Unto all people / she shewed good lyberalyte
Truly fulfyllyng her holy professyon
Theyr fete and handes / wasshyng at the fyrst entre
Of straungers to the place / desyryng them of pardon
Where was no offence / but all thyng well don
Example gyueng / of mekenesse and charyte
Unto all ladyes within christente.

x.

❡ *Of the great affliccion | & hard punysshement that þᵉ*
lady Radegunde vsed aboue the cours of nature
in the sayd tyme of lent.

THis noble princesse mayden Radegunde
A comely quene / a moniall / an abbasse
A floure of vertue / a rose moost rubicunde
Of our lorde was elect / & circumfulsed with grace
To be ruler and lady / of a religyous place
Whose strayte herd penaunce / fame and holynesse
We can nat discrybe nor them expresse

This blessyd abbasse / all the tyme of lenton
Suffred bytter penaunce / & maruelous punysshement
Usyng certayne bandes of yren in custome
Fast knyt to her necke / and armes in chast[is]ment¹
Also .iii. yren chenes / a bout her body went
Full straytely bounde / the holy fast enduryng
To punysshe more pytiously her flesshe freatyng

That whan fortie dayes of lent were past
And the mayde mynded to take them away
The sayd bandes and chenes / remayned so fast
Persyng her body that she ne myght verray

---

¹ PYNSON, *chastment*   *circumfulsed*, shining   *yren*, iron
freatyng, tormenting   *persyng*, piercing   *verray*, indeed

Without great violence / remoue them that day
That blode yssued downe fro the necke / to the fete
In dyuerse parties of her body full wete

She caused to be wrought for greatter penalty
A plate of coper / the sygne of the crosse hauyng
Whiche layed in the fyre / in her cell solitary
She toke the sayd plate / as it was hote brennyng
And layde to her flesshe / as a martyr sufferyng
Punysshyng her corps to bryng it in subiection
Obedient to the soule / by payne and deuocion

This abbasse addyd newe payne vpon payne
In punysshyng her person / more greuously
For why all the lent (sayth the story playne)
Natwithstandyng her vigils / and abstinence openly
She exercysed newe penaunce / and paynes secretly
The heer set with brystels / and yet she vsed more
A chafyngdisshe of coles / to be set her afore

Thus whan she was set / solitary in her cell
Her body quakyng / and her membres all
Dredyng greuous paynes / maruelous to tell
Her soule was armed / to suffre payne temporall
She broyled her body / with the sayd fyre materiall
To anymat / and refresshe the soule in reason
To stand as a martyr / where was no persecucion

Hoote brennyng brasse / she layde to her sydes
Her tender flesshe tremblyng / þe skynne was consumed
The body was combust / with many greuous wondes
The flesshe from the bones / in sundre partȝ deuyded
The blode semydecot to the erthe distylled
Shewyng the verite / of the passyon certayne
Where scilence was kept / for all the greuous payne

semydecot, half cooked

Thus a fragill femynyn / for the loue of Ihesu
Paciently suffred greuous punysshment
Usyng contynually / deuocyon and vertue
Prayer / almisdedes / and charitable feruent
Thorowe which by grace / there folowed incontinent
Myracles (for why) all vayne pleasures transitory
Radegunde refused / myndyng moost our messy.

XI.

❡ *How this holy abbasse vsyng meditacyon refour-*
med her syster neglygent | with a lytell
exortacion folowyng.

THis lady neuer spake / agayne good conscience
She neuer defamed / nor vsed detraccion
Agayne verite / she neuer bare euidence
She neuer dissymuled / nor vsed adulacion
Hastynes / ne yre / debate / nor derysyon
She prayed for her enemyes / to amende by grace
Mouyng her susters / to the same in the place

Great grauite goodnesse / an humilyte
True loue to god / in her hert was feruent
Pacience in aduersyte / faythe / hoope / and charyte
Justyce attemperaunce / fortitude were lent
With prudence benygnite euer resplendent
Gostely example / with good exortacion
Had resydence in Radegunde / and holy religyon

Her example was better / than a commaundement
Unto her subgettes / within the monastery
Her doctryne was profytable / and expedyent
By her fact and dede / she gaue examplary

charitable, charity   *messy*, Messiah   *expedyent*, becoming
examplary, example

Unto her subgettes / and all the famyle
Her precepte and dede / agreed bothe in one
As Christ gaue example / for our saluacyon

Also afore mydnyght moost commenly she sayd
All Dauid psaulter / long before mattence
After whan her systers / in bedde were layed
She styll contynued / prayeng in presence
Of the blessyd sacrementes / departyd nat thence
Tyll the day lyght / knelyng in deuocion
With wepyng teares/ and meke medytacyon

That vnder lycence / and reformacyon
Of all them that this lytell werke shall se
We purpose to reherse / with deuyne proteccyon
Parte of her myracles / folowyng the story
Requiryng all reders / of theyr pure charite
To excuse my ignoraunt boldnesse also
And accept myne entent symple tho it be
Quia bona voluntas / reputetur pro facto

This gracyous Radegunde / ceasyd day nor nyght
Princypally to prayse our lorde / with supplicacyon[1]
Her mynde hert / & mouth / with all her gostly myght
Syngulerly was set her spouse Ihesu vpon
As she was feruent / in her contemplacyon
A moniall Codegunde by a posterne preuatly
Passyd without lycence / out of the monastery

(Whiche thyng knowen) thabbasse folowed shortly
And wolde haue called her by name Codigunda
In stede of whiche name / she sayd veraly
Come agayne dere syster (alleluya alleluya)

---

[1] PYNSON, *supplicacyou*

As the mynde thought / so spake Radegunda
Ryght so it fortuned / after many a season
Her soule was so feruent / vpon meditacion

Swete worthy princesses / borne of great rialte
Duchesses / countesses / ladies euerychone
Folowyng your appetite / and sensualite
In worldly worship / and vayne dilectacion
Diuersite of garmentes made of theyr newe facyon
With delicat dayntes repastyng euery day
The body to conserue / in lust and likyng ay

Beholde and considre with your interiour eye
This humble abbasse / lady and moniall
Howe she refused all wordly dignite
Rychesse / reuerence / and honour imperiall
Vayne / vestures / garmentes / possessyons withall
Entred religion / with great humilite
Truly obseruyng / the essencials thre

Also for sufferyng / in this present lyfe
A lytell whyle payne / for loue of our sauyour
Usyng prayer penaunce / and life contemplatyfe
Nowe she is exalted / in heuenly honour
Whose glory shall euer encrease / more and more
Wherfore noble ladies / example ye may take
At this holy quene / all vice to forsake

O blessyd Radegunde O worthy princesse
Lady and quene / virgyn / and moniall
O vertuous abbasse / and sufferayne maistres
Nowe triumphant / in the see celestiall
We pray the mekely / pray for vs all
That after this lyfe / and mortall passage
We may come to blis / and eterne herytage.

XII.

❡ *Howe blessyd Radegunde delyuered a woman*
possessyd with a fynde | from daunger and
payne | to helth and prosperite.

A Certayne woman dwelled by the monastery
  Whiche was possessyd / with a spirite infernall
By long contynuaunce enduryng misery
Sore vexed / and greued / with paynes thrall
Tearyng with violence / as a beest brutall
Man / woman / and childe / with great cruelte
In a hiduous rage / alas the more pite

Thus she possessyd suffred mycle payne
The mynde sore moued / alienat from reason
The profet of her soule / forgetyng certayne
To charitable werkes / had no entencion
Frewyll was tollyd so was deuocion
She had no power to say nor do truly
But as the sayd fende put in her memory

She was strayte bounde / bothe fote and hande
For drede of myschefe / and wickydnesse
Her frendes dwellyng within the lande
Were woful in hert / no meruell doutlesse
Consideryng theyr kynswoman / in suche distresse
With wepyng waylyng / they came mekely
Besekyng mayde Radegunde / for helpe and remedy

O cumly creature / and kynges doughter dere
O vertuous lady / moniall and abbasse
We call to the knelyng afore the here
Haue pyte and compassyon / in this extreme case
Be thou our succour / comfort and solace
Helpe this wofull wreche / humble we the pray
By thy prayer and myght as thou well may

Unto whose prayer peticyon and desyre
Saynt Radegunde / was moued to compassyon
Commaundyng them all / with loue entyre
To bryng the sayd woman / and wofull person
Unto her presence / hastely and soone
Her frendes were glad / and made good chere
Ioyfull to fulfyll the commaundement in fere

Whan they aproched / to this wofull pacient
Redy to conuey her / to the holy place
The sayd wickyd spyryte[1] / moued her entent
Euer to the contrary / by power and manace
She rayled / and raged / and spyt in theyr face
At the last by power / and wysdome and myght
This woman was brought / before this lady bryght

On whom she had compassion / and pety
And anone commaunded / in presence of them all
That wycked sprite / and mortall enemy
To cease of his greuance / and paynes thrall
And shortly to the grounde / before her to fall
Also to departe this sayd woman fro
Neuer more to vex her with payne nor wo

Anone the sprite obeyed / the commaundement
Myght no lenger tary / day nor yet houre
Immediatly departed / from the feble pacient
With an hydeous cry full of great doloure
The woman rose vp out of her langour
And kneled downe / thankyng god almyght
And blessed Radegunde of this myracle ryght

---

[1] PYNSON, *sporyte*

XIII.

℃ *Howe a ratte was slayne without hande apro-*
chyng to hurt the vertuous labour
of saynt Radegund.

This abbasse vsed somtyme meditacion
Somtyme prayer / vigils / and abstinence
Whylom in labours / & wordly occupacion
The tyme to dispend / in vertuous excellence
And as my auctour gyueth intellygence
This lady had wrought / with great besynesse
A clew of yarne in auoyding ydelnesse

Whiche clew Radegunde hange forthe in the son
At her chamber windo to take ayre and dry
And anone theyr came a myghty great ratton
Aprochyng the yarne to gnawe it / and destry
But as soone as she touched the clewe certenly
In the fyrst morsell she fell to grounde deed
Without mannes hand (in story as is reed)

XIV.

℃ *Howe saynt Radegunde by prayer reuiued a lau-*
rell tre to burge and bryng forthe leaues
without any rote.

This venerable virgyn commaunded also
Her seruauntz to remoue a great laurell tre
Ferre from the place where it did gro
To set it securly within the monastere
Ryght afore her cell / to comfort the company
Whiche laurell tre / by the rote cut a way
Was brought / and transplanted into a garden gay

The sayd laurell tre without rote whiche was
Began soone to fade / to wyder / and to dry
The leaues fell a downe of pleasure / and solace
Nature in it decayed / and no meruell securly
But whan the virgyn perceyued it truly
She supposed and imputed all to her person
Cause of negligence / or want of deuocion

Than Radegunde began mekely for to pray
That the sayd laurell myght reuiued be
And anone by myracle / the same selfe day
The tre newly burgened / pleasaunt for to se
And brought forthe leaues vernant in suauite
With fresshe fayre braunches / couering the grounde
The tre had a newe rote / as it was tried and founde.

xv.

℘ *Howe saynt Radegunde by humble intercession*
restored a yong Nunne from dethe
to lyfe agayne.

ANother season / whan this holy abbasse
Was in her cell vsyng meditacion
She herd a great wepyng / & crieng alas
Among the seruantes / & congregacion
The cause was this by playne demonstracyon
A vertuous syster / a yong moniall
That tyme departed from this lyfe mortall

Radegunde vp rose full spedely
To comfort the company / with compassyon
Desiryng the seruantes / to bryng the deed body
Secretly to her cell / and solitary mansion
After she commaunded them / all and one
Without any taryeng to depart theyr way
Unto theyr besynesse / and for the soule to pray

Whan all thyng was redy for the buriall
In mean tyme Radegund prayed our sauyour
By space of .vii. houres for this yong moniall
Unto the body the sprite for to restore
Whose prayer endyd the soule that same houre
Reuerted to the corps / restored to lyfe agayne
Cured from all sekenes / vexacion / and payne.

XVI.

❡ *Howe saynt Radegunde saued her seruantes from*
paryll of perisshyng which brought a parte
of the holy crosse to Pectauis.

THis vertuous abbasse / send to the emperoure
Of Constantynople for a porcion
Of the holy crosse / on whome our sauyour
For vs suffred deth / and payed our raunsom
The messangers opteyned theyr meke peticion
Receyued a litell part of the crosse certayne
From thens departyd / to theyr lady agayne

And as they passed / saylyng on the see
Sodenly rose vp wyndes moste hideous
The ayre forderkened by craft of our enemy
Great stormes aproched myghty / and meruelous
The tempest encreasyd / euen more greuous
The maryners were besy in eche part to attende
And laboured full fast theyr lyues to amende

The stormes and tempestis / continued truly
Fortie dayes and fortie nyghtes / withouten ceasyng
The mariners were mased mated / and wery
The ship was euer in parell of perysshyng

---

amende, **save**   *mased,* bewildered   *mated,* perplexed

So whan the messangers knewe no other thyng
But deth approchyng of theyr lyues desperate
They called on Radegund / & sayd with mynde eleuate

O louely lady and blessed abbasse
O holy virgyn / and kynges doughter dere
O vertuous moniall replete with great grace
Helpe nowe thy seruauntes from paryll and dangere
Defende vs from deth / which aprocheth nere
Ceasse these great sees O swete maistres
Spede vs in our Iorney / thorowe thy goodnes

Suffre neuer the enemy of all mankynde
By malyce and enuy / to drenche vs all
Also swete lady / call to thy mynde
That we haue nowe brought / a relique speciall
And don well our message / by grace supernall
Therfore madame / in this necessite
Pray for vs all / to the blessyd trinyte

Ryght shortly apperyd / in all theyr syght
A whyte doufe flyeng / the ship all about
The tempest ceasyd / by myracle right
The wyndes were layde / within and without
The see was quiet / withouten dout
The marchandes / the maryners / with voyce Iocunde
Magnyfied our maker / and mayden Radegunde

The messangers came whome / all in prosperyte
And brought with them / the relique / of reuerence
Whiche solemply was set / in the monastery
With honour / worshyp / and mycle dilygence
And whan it came to open syght and presence
Myracles were shewed / by it euery day
Unto the people / of the sayd countray

doufe, dove   *whome*, home

XVII.

❡ *Of dyuerse myracles in generall | and how this*
abbasse saued dyuerse seke persons from
Ieopardy of deth.

WHat memory or reason is sufficient
To remember the myracles of this lady
What tong can expresse / or pen is conuenient
Playnly to describe / all the noble story
It were a pleasaunt werke for the monke of Bury
For Chaucer or Skelton / fathers of eloquens
Or for religious Barkeley to shewe theyr diligens

yet vnder licence / speke we in generall
Part of the myracles / of this virgyn bright
Where a sicke man in slepe by monicion speciall
Receyued of Radegunde a candell lyght
Soon after by her grace / comfort and myght
He was well cured from all infyrmite
Restored to helth / and to prosperite

Also a nother man feble and impotent
Endured suche sickenesse / and debylite
That by the space of .x. dayes consequent
He toke no sustenaunce / meate nor drynke truly
To whome this mayden (of her great charite)
Came for to visyt / and the pacient anone
Cured from sickenes / receyued refection.

---

the monke of Bury, John Lydgate   *monicion,* vision
consequent, subsequently

XVIII.

❧ *How Radegunde thabbasse cured .ii. sycke women
from sickenesse | and infyrmite vnto helth
and prosperyte.*

A Noble gentillwoman Bella nominat
    Wyfe vnto Gylbard / of the realme of Fraunce
With sundry sickenesse / and blyndnesse cruciat
Long tyme enduryng / suche wofull penaunce
Was brought to Radegunde / for helpe of her greuans
Her frendes wofull pensyue in mynde
Desyred this virgyn / for to helpe the blynde

This abbasse replete / with grace and pitie
Signed this woman / vnto our sauyour
With the signe of the crosse / for helpe and remedy
Makyng intercession / for her that houre
The sicke was delyuerd / from payne and langoure
Cured from blyndnes / had her sight agayne
She thankyd our lorde / and Radegunde certayne

Also a nother woman / was cured from payne
By merite of this mayde / and singuler supplicacion
Hauyng a great byle / by twene her shulders twayne
Of long continuaunce / full of corrupcion
For the wofull woman / she made intercissyon
Unto our sauyour / and kyng of mercy
To sende her helth / helpe and remedy

And whan the sayd orison endyd was
This swollyn bonche horrible to nature
Dyd braste a sundre / with the skyn in that place
A worme yssued out of a great stature
Whiche was distroyed afore them full sure
The pacient was healed / from payne in sight
By grace aboue kynd / and myracle right.

cruciat, tormented   *bonche,* tumour   *braste,* burst

XIX.

❡ *How this abbasse healed dyuerse sicke women som*
from feuers | and some from vexacion
of our gostly enemy.

A Certayne deuout religious moniall
    Was vexed all þe day with great colnesse
And in the nyght tyme / with hete ouer all
As a feruent feuer / of wo & paynfulnesse
That she myght nat serue / our lorde god doutlesse
Nother nyght nor day / for sore vexacion
Whiche was to her soule / a dowble tribulacion

This blessyd mayden / replete with grace certayne
Commaunded warme water / to be had in hye
Which water she touched / with her handes twayne
Gaue it to her syster / the payne to mortyfy
So whan she touched / the sayd sycke body
The moniall receyued helth and prosperite
Cured from all qualites / of suche contrariete

A nother woman long had in possessyon
Of a wickyd sprite prostrat / in the pauement
Was brought to this mayde for preseruacion
On whome she had pyte / and prayde full delygent
Our lorde to delyuer the spyrite from the pacient
She blessyd this woman / and the deuell right sure
Departyd shortly / by the secretis of nature

A certayne mayden dwellyng in Fraunce
Nominat Roda was vexed day and nyght
With the colde feuers / and paynefull greuance
Whiche mekely was mesured / to this lady bryght
By whose humble orison all payne ceassyd right
The feuers were fled / helth aproched nere
Or the candell was endyd / sayth the story clere

hye, haste   *had*, held   *or*, before

A religyous abbasse / manassyd full sore
Blessyd Radegunde excom*m*unicat to be
Except she wolde heele / and saue from langore
A woman possessyd / with a spyrite paynefully
By grace so it fortuned / that within dayes thre
Our olde aduersary / departyd her fro
The woman was delyuerd / from payne & gostly wo.

xx.

℄ *Of the gostly visyon she had afore her infyrmyte &*
of the noble exortacion she made to her
systers in her skyenes & payne.

𝔑Owe to the glorious passage / of this abbasse
Passe we with gladnesse / and felicite
Whiche in her tyme / was a floure of grace
An example of vertue / and benygnite
A myrour of mekenes / and pure chastite
A vertuous gouernour / of her congregacion
To bryng them to glory / and heuenly mansyon

Suche grace she optayned / of our sauyour
That afore her passage / a hole yere full right
Our lorde sende his angell / with mycle honour
To be her comfort / helpe day and nyght
The angell aperyd / to this lady bryght
In fourme of a yong man / moost fayre to be tolde
Whiche gladdyd her soule / and mynde manyfolde

The angell shewed Radegunde in vision
A glorious place / in the celestyall see
Prepared for her / to haue fruicion
Where ioy is infinite / and endles glory
Rehersyng these wordes / with great Iocundite
O glorious abbasse / quene and moniall
Our lorde to the sendyth / gretyng speciall

to be tolde, sic PYNSON; *? to be holde*

Shewyng howe / for thy vertu and mekenesse
Thy vigils / fastynges / and deuocion
Thy wepynges / waylinges / and tendernesse
Thy bytter penaunce / and sharpe affliction
Thou shalt haue merite / and glorificacion
And in my diadem thou shalt sure be
A precious gemme / resplendent with beaute

Swete virgyn to the I playnly expresse
To Iesu thy spouse / thou shalt come hastely
From wordly vexacion / payne and besenesse
To abyde and endure / in ioy perpetually
Whiche singuler comfort / and visyon gostly
Secretly she shewed vnto systers twayne
Vertuous in lyuyng / suche grace to optayne

Sone after this sayd gostly reuelacion
Sickenes approched her and infirmite
The messanger of deth / and wordly seperacion
Dayly increasyd with wo and penalyte
Her body was brought to suche debilyte
That she sore dred her lyfe euery day
The panges and passions doubled alway

As she endured suche langore and sickenes
She send for her systers / and all the couent
Exortyng them to vertu and goodnesse
Principally to kepe our lordes commaundment
With gostly perfection / and be euer pacient
Use mekenesse in hert / and true charite
With loue vnto god / from the hert fre

She sayd dere systers / I pray you euerychone
Dayly to obserue the essencials thre
Of saynt Benettes rule / your holy religion
Parfyt obedience / and wylfull pouerte

With the floure of clennesse and pure chastite
Kepe your doctrines / and customes sperituall
With gostly obseruantes / and cerimonies all

Honour and loue our lorde aboue all thyng
Occupy the tyme in meditacion
In deuout prayer and discrete fastyng
In vigils penaunce / and contemplacion
Call vnto mynde your strayte profession
Obserue the order ye be professyd vnto
Remembre this lesson / what so euer ye do

Also my counsell is / that ye shalbe content
With the visitacion of god all myghty
Whether he send you pleasure or punysshement
Quietnes vexacion helth or infirmite
For this ye knowe / by his auctorite
The childe whome the father loueth most dere
He doth most punysshe tenderly in fere.

XXI.

❡ *With what pacience and deuocion lady Radegund*
receyued þe blessyd sacrament & extreme vnction
afore her departure

After ward she askyd the holy communion
With mycle reuerence / and humilite
To comfort the soule agayne temptacion
At the sharpe passage / of this mortalyte
Where preistes / and clarkes / were all redy
Theyr offyce to supple right conuenient
And brought with them / the blessyd sacrament

supple, fulfil   *conuenient,* becomingly

At whose commyng / this reuerent Radegunde
With gostly comfort humbled her body
Sayeng to the sacrament / with hert iocunde
Welcome my maker / god sonne almighty
Welcom my redemer / and kyng of glory
Welcom my ioy / comfort and solace
My trust / my treasure / in euery place

As the church techith / I beleue stydfastly
That thou descendyd from blis eternall
And was incarnat / in mayden Mary
Suffred passyon / and deth moost thrall
Man soule to redeme / from payne infernall
And that thou institute / thy blessyd body
In furme of bredde to vs sacramentally

Thus with great wepyng / and feruent deuocion
In true fayth / hope / and charite
Radegunde receyued the holy communion
To preserue the soule from ieopardy
With all obseruance / and suffrage gostly
After all this she askyd extreme vnction
For spirituall comfort / and saluacyon

And as she lay in suche extremite
Sufferyng great payne / abydyng the houre
She be toke her soule / vnto the custodie
Of Ihesu her spouse / our blessyd sauyour
Also to visyt her / they came with great honoure
Many sad citesyns wyddowes / virgyns pure
Lamentyng and wepyng / for her departure

They held vp theyr handes / towarde heuen on hye
Pyteously cryeng / made great lamentacion
Sayeng O blessyd lorde / god almyghty
Why suffers thou this mayde / departe from vs alon

thrall, severe

Fatherles childerne without consolacion
Good lorde if it be thy wyll and pleasure
Permyt her to abyde with vs and endure

O blessyd abbasse / thou art our succoure
Our singuler comfort / both day and nyght
Our helpe and refuge / agayne all langoure
Our speciall defence / vnder god almyght
Alas swete maistres / and lady bryght
Why wyll you departe / from vs so hastely
But agayne deth / may be no remedy.

XXII.

℃ *Of the departure of this holy abbasse / and howe she*
apperyd þe same houre to a noble prefect / curyng
hym from sickenesse of his throte.

THis venerable virgyn / expired sothely
The .xiii. day of August / to blis eternall
Angels were present / with mycle melody
To receyue the soule / from the lyfe temperall
For euer to reigne / in the see celestiall
To haue her merite / and glorificacion
For her great vertue / and contemplacion

And at the same houre / of her departyng
Quareours laboryng / in the mounte therby
Herd swete armony of angels singyng
One sayd howe the voyce of a sad company
Ascendeth to the eares of god almyghty
Suffre her no lenger to endure distres
Take her to ioy / and eterne quietnes

Whan the angels sayeng / thus endyd was
They receyued the soule / of this fayre lady
And brought it syngyng / to the celestiall palace
(As afore is sayd) to reigne eternally
Unto whiche place / of endles glory
Pray for vs abbasse / and holy moniall
That we may thyder come / both one and all

Manyfolde merites / and myracles memoratyue
Magnifien this mayde / with great magnificence
Enduryng the tyme / of this present lyfe
And at her departure / knowen by experience
For she apperyd gostly in presence
The same houre she passyd / from this lyfe dolorous
To a great gouernoure / called Demolemus

This sayd Demolemus / was paynfully cruciat
In his brest and throte / by host and swellyng
His breth restrayned with passyons tortuat
Ryght like to expire / at euery hours endyng
Radegunde bad hym / straytely commaundyng
To lose .iii. presoners / within his Iayle and holde
And he shulde haue helth / and pleasure manyfolde

(Whiche visyon past) he waked sodenly
Callyng to mynde / her wyll and commaundement
Knewe well by the visyon / that this noble lady
Than was departed from this lyfe present
Prouyng the trueth / by messangers diligent
Afterwarde he sende his seruant to the prison
Deliuerd all captyue from payne and affliction

Incontynently by merit and grace of this abbasse
Demolemus mended / of sickenes and infyrmite
His throte and his heed / whiche wofull was
Were sone delyuered / from all penalyte

memoratyue, memorable   *host*, cough

His breth restored / at his owne lyberte
This forsayd ruler / and the prisoners all
Praysed this virgyn / with mynde speciall

Whiche sayd myracles notyfied playne
Thorowe the countrey / and all the region
Many poore prisoners / sufferyng great payne
Made dayly prayers / and humble supplicacion
Unto this lady promisyng an oblacion
Desiryng her suffrage with humylite
Were saued from deth / and put at lyberte.

XXIII.

❧ *How saynt Radegund cured one of her seruantes*
from the plage of fier sittyng in her chayer
without auctorite and right.

SOone after the departure of this pure virgin
A woman of Uiuoberga one of her famylye
Of hye ambicion willyng to domyn
Sat in her chayer / right presumptuously
Commendyng her selfe / that place moost worthy
So whan she had done / this offence greuous
The punysshement of god / fell on her dolorous

Her body brenned / as doth a hote furnace
The fyer[1] ascended / to the ayre on hye
The payne continued / and neuer ceassed was
Thre dayes and .iii. nyghtes / induryng feruently
This wofull woman seyng no remedy
With hert penitent / made playne confession
Of her euyll dede and hye presumpcion

---

[1] PYNSON, *finde.*   *domyn*, rule
of Uiuoberga—a mistranslation of Antoninus' "Uiuoberga una eius
famula fuit."

She sayd swete Radegunde / haue pitie on me
O comly quene / forgyue me myn offence
Ceasse this feruent plage / I pray to the
Pardon my pryde / and great negligence
I haue offended / your hye prehemynence
And euill trespased / agaynst your hye honoure
Saue me swete lady / from payne and doloure

Also the people / on her had compassyon
Tenderly for her / prayde knelyng on kne
Unto our sauyour / with hye deuocion
And to saynt Radegunde / her helpe to be
Anone this virgyn / on her hauyng pite
Ceassed this feruent fyer of punysshement
This woman was saued / and cured from torment.

XXIV.

❡ *A breue rehersall of the great profet and remedy
founde by true oblacion made to this moniall.*

These forsayd myracles / and other many one
Infinite to reherse all seriously
This virgin shewed / by singuler deuocion
Unto all people sicke and in miserye
Desiryng her prayers / and suffrages mekely
All suche departed from her with gladnesse
Whiche came to her presence / in wo and heuenesse

Among all myracles after our intelligence
Whiche Radegunde shewed by her humilite
One is moost vsuall had in experience
Among the common people / noted with hert fre
By offeryng of otes / after theyr degre
At her holy aulters where myracles in sight
Dayly haue be done by grace day and nyght

By oblacion of othes / halt / lame / and blynde
Hath ben restored / vnto prosperite
Dombe men to speke / aboue cours of kynde
Sickemen delyuered / from payne and miserie
Maydens hath kept theyr pure virginite
Wyddowes defended from greuous oppression
And clarkes exalted / by her to promocion

Many other myracles / she shewed expresse
To euery estate / religious and rurall
By her great vertue / merite / and goodnesse
Whiche be nat rehersed / here in speciall
But who so lyst to knowe her myracles all
May forther enquire / of theyr benignite
The boke of her myracles where in they written be

Whiche miracles / who redeth ceriously
Marke / mynde / and bere them well away
Shall fynde that our lorde god / the kyng of glory
Sheweth his myghty power day by day
For all suche: whiche in theyr hartes fynde may
Hym to loue / and serue aboue all thynge
And hym to folowe / gladly in theyr lyuynge

Lyke as dyd / this virgyn pudicall
As in her lyfe I haue made mencion
She forsoke the pleasures / great and small
Of this worlde: and set all her affection
Porely to lyue in strayte religion
In prayer / fastyng / and worthy penaunce
With watche / labour / and simple sustinaunce

She viseted the sicke persons impotent
And ministred / with good hert and mynde
To them such thynges / as were conuenient
She succurred both lame / halte / and blynde

othes, oats   *rurall*, lay

And the sore lazers / where she dyd them fynde
She wasshed / and touched theyr sores tenderly
And neuer abhorred / any malady

Her almes she gaue / there as she sawe nede
To monasteries / and persons religious
Brefely to speke / many a vertuous dede
She fulfylled: for whiche our lorde Iesus
For her shewed suche miracles glorious
What tyme she was here in this worlde lyuyng
And also syth her hens away partynge

XXV.

❦ *A prayer or orison of the blessyd quene*
Radegunde moniall and abbasse.

Noble princesse / flouryng in vertue
Borne of kyngȝ blodde / by course of nature
O blessyd Radegunde the spouses of Iesu
A myrour of mekenesse / to euery creature
In thy yong age / refusyng wordly pleasure
Nowe reignest in heuen / and ioy lastyng ay
We the beseke / swete virgyn pure
Preserue and defende vs both nyght and day

O comly quene / and lady excellent
Somtyme vnder spousage / lyueng in chastite
Entendyng for to please our lorde omnipotent
And the worlde refuse with all vanite
A wyfe and a mayde as fewe other be
Weryng the herd heare vnder garmentes gay
At our departure of thy benignite
Preserue and defende vs both nyght and day

Thy chast conuersacion vnder matrimonye
Euer entended holy perfeccion
Dayly fulfillyng the werkesse of mercye
And vpon the poore hauing compassion
Releuing prisoners in wofull affliccion
Most mercifull princesse proued all way
We the require / with humble supplicacion
Preserue and defende vs both nyght and day

And whan thou was in holy religion
Thou shewed example of humilite
To all thy systers / and congregacion
Howe they shulde kepe theyr chastite
Theyr true profession / the essencials thre
A lanterne of light / shening verray
Wherfore we pray the of thy charite
Preserue and defende vs both nyght and day

Euery creature in this present lyfe
May take of the parfyt imitacion
Both quene and princesse / lady and wyfe
Remembring thy straytenesse in religion
Thy prayers / penaunce / vigils / meditacion
The torment of thy body / without delay
In euery tyme namely in lenton
Preserue and defende vs both nyght and day

Also for thy vertue and great holynesse
Many myracles were shewed both day and nyght
People were cured / by the from sickenesse
Halt and lame heled / blynd had theyr sight
Impotent persons / restored to myght
Wickyd sprites abiecte / it is no nay
Of thy great charite swete lady bright
Preserue and defende vs both nygh[t][1] and day

[1] PYNSON, *nygh.*

O beauteous gemme and saphyre celestiall
O worthy diamounde / shening with honour[1]
In the heuenly troune with ioy angelicall
Praysing and louyng our blessed sauyour
Make thou intercession / sheweng thy deuour
For vs thy seruauntes / as thou well may
Namely at this tyme / and at euery houre
Preserue and defende vs / both nyght and day

O rubicunde rose vernant in pulcritude
Our dayly comfort / plesant to be holde
O lylly whyte floure / shenyng with claritude
O radiant ster / passyng perle and golde
Our singuler defence / and succoure to be tolde
To thy spouse Iesu / for vs thou daily pray
That we may repent / our synne manyfolde
Preserue and defende vs both nyght and day

For vs make instaunce / O gracious lady
O quene and princesse / moniall and abbasse
That we may optayne here pardon and mercy
And clere be absolued / from synne and trespasse
And after this lyfe / to se the glorious face
Of the blessyd trinite / in blis to our pay
Where ioy is infinite / and eternall grace
Helpe virgyn Radegunde / both nyght and day.

[1] PYNSON, *houour*.   *deuour*, regard   *pay*, satisfaction

XXVI.

❧ *A breue conclucyon / & end of this poore translacyon*
mouyng the reders to accept this lytell [boke][1]
vnworthy to be redde.

Ere beloued brother / in our lorde Iesu
My faythfull louer / and speciall frynde
Glad I am to know your goodnes & vertu
To whome with humilite I me recommend
shewyng to you þᵗ I haue brought to end
And translate in to englisshe / the noble story
Of mayden Radegunde as ye desyred me

Requiryng you tenderly of your gentilnes
To accept this present poore translacion
Excusyng my ignoraunce / and symplenesse
Takyng my mynde / and humble intention
Whiche warke is done / of no presumption
Also pardon my termes though they rude be
Frutles of sentence full of prolixite

Nowe to all poetis flouryng moost eloquent
And to all other / that this lyfe shall rede or se
With humble submission / I do it represent
Desiryng them all / of theyr charite
To correct and reforme it where is necessite
Which sayd translacion / and indigne werke
Is for common people / written for no clerke

And where this virgyn / and gracious lady
Hath be kept scilent and close a long season
Knowen to fewe persons / within this countrey
Therefore we purposed / vnder her proteccion
To declare her lyfe and gostly conuersacion

---

[1] Omitted by PYNSON.

Dilatyng her fame / and shewe her excellence
Extollyng her name with great magnificence

Euery great estate / empresse / quene / and duchesse
Example may take at this moniall
To encrease in vertu / and proued mekenesse
In churche to be deuout / and courtesse in hall
And to the poore people for to be liberall
Euery true matrone her doctrine folowyng
In heuen may be sure to haue a wonnyng

And who so that is a person religious
May lerne at this lady to kepe pacience
To be humble in soule / gentyll and vertuous
Obseruyng chastite / and true obedience
With wilfull pouerte / without concupiscence
And euer content be with what Iesu doth sende
yeuyng humble thankes vnto your lyues end.

Go fourth lytell boke / blacke be thy vesture
As euer mournyng inable to come to lyght
Submit the also vnto euery creature
Whiche reason hath desiryng to haue a sight
O blessyd sauyour / and lorde moost of myght
Preserue this poore boke from hate and enmyte
With all humble reders of thy benignite.

∴   *Amen.*   ∴

❡ *Thus endeth the lyfe of saynt Radegunde Im-*
printed by Rycharde Pynson printer
to the kynges noble grace Cum
priuilegio a rege
indulto.
∵

wonnyng, dwelling

9 781107 415928